There's Something About ROBINS

By Nick Vakalopoulos

Briley & Baxter Publications | Plymouth, Massachusetts

Hardcover ISBN: 978-1-954819-97-9
Paperback ISBN: 978-1-961978-03-4

Book Design: Stacy Padula

Dedication

To my Father and Mother, Harry and Mary.

To my dear friends Paul, Susan, Jack, Carol
and the entire Alexopoulos family.

Above all, to the Author of the Universe.
For prompting me to bring this work forth.

There's something about Robins.

The way they hop.

The way they stop.

The way they look.

The way they listen.

The way they search the earth
for worms that glisten.

They poke and prod the ground with might.

Then catch a worm or bug in sight.

They run and stall when worms will crawl.

Then do their best to catch them all.

They eat their meal in one whole bite.

And then take flight with feathers bright.

They zig and zag across the grass.

With will and zest their time does pass.

They feed their young with much love and care.

Real soon, one day, they'll take to the air.

Worms try hard to get away.

But alas, it's not their day!

There's something about Robins.

Something about Robins alright.

My favorite bird and great delight!

Something About the Author

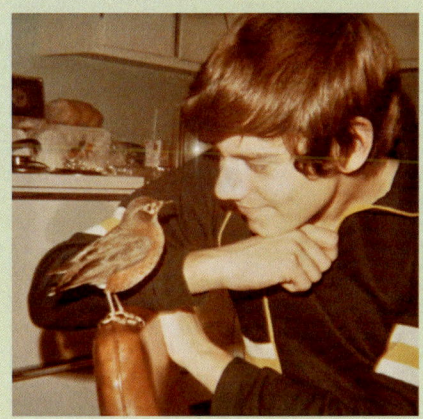

One spring day when I was fourteen years old, a little girl from our neighborhood was walking down our street. In her hands she was carrying a large box. When she saw me in my parent's backyard, she approached me and said: "I found this baby bird on the ground and I don't know what to do with it. Will you take it for me?"

Well for sure that's not what I had planned for the day but for some reason, I agreed. She left, and without knowing where the nest was, I asked my parent's permission if we could try and raise the little bird. It just so happened to be a baby Robin. When it was strong, healthy, and able to fly we released it back into the wild where it belonged. Ever since then, the Robin has been and will remain my favorite bird.

Now as a wildlife photographer, I've had a special interest in capturing photos of Robins in action for many years. Observing all of their movements and habits prompted me to write the words in this book. Also, the photos featured in the book were processed through a computer art filter to give them a painterly quality. This creative venture came about in a divine and organic way over a long time. My hope is that this book inspires a sense of wonderment and reverence not just for Robins, but for all of nature and creation.

www.ingramcontent.com/pod-product-compliance
Lightning Source LLC
Chambersburg PA
CBRC090839120626
46551CB00008B/707